THE POETESS OF AUSCHWITZ

and

THE BOY WITH SIX NAMES

Copyright © 2023 by Alexandra Hays

All rights reserved. No part of this book may be reproduced or transmitted in any form or by any means, electronic or mechanical, including photocopying, recording, or by any information storage or retrieval system, without written permission from the author.

Cover and Layout Design: Lazar Kackarovski

ISBN: 979-8-373832-81-6

First edition January 2023

The POETESS OF AUSCHWITZ *and* THE BOY WITH SIX NAMES

ALEXANDRA HAYS

For Jerry

"I will never be as jubilant as when I found out my child was still alive."

• Eva Pomeranz •

CONTENTS

Chapter 1: Henrich 1

Chapter 2: Smuggling 11

Chapter 3: Captivity 13

Chapter 4: Poetess 25

Chapter 5: Juraj 33

Chapter 6: Internment 39

Chapter 7: The Rabbi 51

Chapter 8: The castle 59

Chapter 9: Homecoming 67

AUTHOR'S NOTE 71

ACKNOWLEDGEMENTS 75

REFERENCES 77

ABOUT THE AUTHOR 79

1

HENRICH

Bratislava, Slovakia
• 1941 •

Gisela Pomeranz (also spelled "Pomerantz" on German documents and "Ewa Pommeranz" on Polish documents) was born in Tarnów, Poland on February 20, 1922. While her childhood was typical for a Jewish girl of that era, nothing in her upbringing could've prepared her for the turns her life would take.

Gisela was never fond of her first name and went by the name "Eva." Tarnów, a small city near Kraków, was home to about 25,000 Jewish inhabitants before World War II—roughly half of the city's population (United States Holocaust Memorial Museum).

Eva, whose mother died when she was seven, had one younger brother, Salo, and a sister Hannah, or "Anna," twelve years her senior. Eva was close with her maternal grandmother and would spend summers with her before the War.

Not much more is known about Eva's early years in Poland as the events of WW II overshadowed her childhood. On September 7, 1939, when Eva was seventeen, German soldiers invaded Tarnów and began harassing the city's Jewish population. Two months later, the Germans had destroyed nearly all of the city's synagogues. On November 23, 1939, it was decreed that all Jewish citizens over the age of eleven in Nazi-occupied Poland must wear a Star of David badge on their right arm, with severe consequences for failed compliance. With chaos around them, the Pomeranz family knew they were not safe.

Under persecution, some Jewish families in Europe fled to locations they believed to be safer while others stayed put, convinced they could withstand the hardships to come, and the anti-Semitic restrictions would soon be reversed.

While it isn't clear exactly how, Eva escaped the oppressive conditions in Tarnów without the rest of her family. Roundups and pogroms had already begun, and it was after one of these actions the majority of Eva's family was taken, perhaps when she was away at school. Eva, finding herself alone and in danger of being seized by the Germans, fled across the border of Slovakia without any official paperwork.

Young Eva found herself in Žilina, Slovakia, and landed refuge working in an elderly Jewish woman's house. The social climate in Slovakia at the time only allowed Jews to find employment working for other Jews. The relative safety Eva found in Žilina was short-lived, as soon non-Jewish neighbors began asking about Eva's identity. Her employer suggested that Eva flee to the Slovakian capital, Bratislava, where she arranged for Eva to work in her daughter's household as domestic help. The woman suggested a new face might not attract attention in the bigger border city. Eva relocated to the capital and settled in with the Engel family—Arnost Engel and his wife—at Recna 2 in Bratislava. Mr. Engel owned a coffee exporting company called Eco Co., which supported many employees. During this time Eva also worked at a Jewish kindergarten.

It was shortly after her arrival in Bratislava that Eva met and fell in love with a young man. While further confirmation was never found about the man who won Eva's affections, there is one document that names him as "Frantisek Kohn." If that document is accurate, the limited information on Frantisek Kohn lists him as a fellow Jewish refugee from Nitra, Slovakia who landed in Bratislava where he worked in a factory doing electrical work. Eva and her beau fell in love in 1939-1940, but without official papers permitting their residence in Slovakia, and more importantly being Jewish, they could not register to marry at any government building without bringing undue danger upon themselves. So, it is believed that Eva and Frantisek lived together as if they were a married couple, and a pregnancy soon followed.

It is important to underscore the social and political climate in Slovakia at the outbreak of WWII and what that meant for newly-pregnant Eva.

During the war, Slovakia became a newly-independent state with two masters: Germany and the Vatican.

Slovakian lands, which had been part of the First Czechoslovak Republic from 1918 until 1938, broke away and emerged as a new pseudo-independent state backed by Germany. This move towards a nationalist Slovak nation was backed by the Slovak People's Party: a far-right national political party originally headed by a Catholic priest, Andrei Hlinka. As Slovakians at the time were predominantly practicing Catholics (about eighty percent of the population), priests had great influence in the country. As a testament to the confidence entrusted to clergy, in Slovakia's newly-formed parliament, 16 of 63 seats were taken by priests.

However, there was infighting in Slovakia as to how the newly-formed nation's government should operate and what allegiances it should hold. For every move toward a closer relationship with Germany, there was opposition from moderates within the country.

Nevertheless, upon Hlinka's death in 1938, Catholic priest Jozef Tiso was installed as Hlinka's successor as prime minister of Slovakia. Tiso was later named president. Tiso's personal antisemitism is documented, including in a speech in 1942 where he called Jews "parasites" and the "eternal enemy."

Under Tiso's leadership, Slovakia adopted the "Jewish Code" in 1941, which listed 270 measures aimed at Slovakia's Jewish population that forbade Jews from owning land, excluded them from public office and certain occupations, expelled them from schools and universities, and compelled all Jews to wear yellow Star of David armbands in public.

Slovakia was the first German ally to agree to Jewish deportations in support of the "Final Solution," and deportations of Slovakia's Jewish population began in 1942. The new Slovak government entered into an agreement to pay Germany 500 Reichsmarks for every Jew "relocated" to Nazi territory. This payment was in part to guarantee disenfranchised Jews would not return to Slovakia or make future claims on their commandeered property.

The commands of Tiso's government were carried out by an elite, far-right armed organization called the Hlinka Guard. The Guard's aim was to "safeguard and promote the national life of the Slovak people and to fight the enemies of Slovak national, social, political, and religious life," (Conway, 1974). In reality, the Guard was an armed militia with the backing of a ruling political party which assaulted Jews in public, confiscated Jewish property for personal gain, and were the enforcement arm of rounding up Slovakia's Jewish population for deportation to concentration camps. The Hlinka Guards were not above murder as evidenced by the Kremnička and Nemecká massacres, where Guards killed more than 700 people in cooperation with German death squad troops.

Throughout the War, although the government became aligned with Germany, the people of Slovakia were not of a single accord. There were concerns from some of the citizenry and also some clergy that history would look poorly on Slovakia's treatment of Jews. Many Catholic priests opposed the regime's treatment of Slovakia's Jewish population and wrote to Rome on their behalf. For example, the Vicar of Bratislava wrote letters pleading for the Vatican to intervene, as did the Bishop of Prešov, who headed the Byzantine-Catholic Church in Slovakia. Catholicism, it seems, was at war with itself in Slovakia.

While there is mixed opinion on Pope Pius XII's official stance on the plight of the Jewish population in Europe, correspondence from the Vatican does exist condemning antisemitism and the deportation of Jews. It is worth noting that in neighboring Hungary, the Catholic leadership staunchly opposed the Nazis and their policies—a very different climate than in Slovakia. It is clear that individual Catholic clergy and citizens, from repeated anecdotes throughout Europe, often risked everything to hide and protect Jews from deportation.

It was in this tense social climate that Eva gave birth to a baby boy on September 6, 1941, and gave him the name Henrich Jurji. The child had ashen-brown hair, a pronounced nose, and big, hazel eyes.

Accounts from acquaintances noted that the baby's father was taken away by authorities only a few months after Henrich was born, very early in 1942. Eva was left alone with an infant in a country that politically aligned itself with the Nazis.

Not long after her beau's capture, Eva and her young son were forced into the Bratislava ghetto. It was crowded, food was scarce, and rumors of what would happen to the Jews who were forced there were plentiful. All that is known about Eva's emotional state during this pivotal time in her life is captured in eleven original poems that have previously never been published as an ensemble.

I Am Longing

In the late hours of the day
As my thoughts turn to you
From the wound in my heart
A silent, secret feeling flows.
I see you as if it was yesterday
With a compassionate smile on your face,
Therefore for you I am writing this poem.
All that we experienced together was wonderful
As if I was reading a love story
And my heart was quietly shivering.
Today it is all just part of a dream
A beautiful dream of the past.
Deeply driven into my thoughts
Remains a quiet suffering in the heart.

My Dream

This morning while I was still asleep
I received your roses and your letter,
On it, tightly-scrawled on all four pages
A thousand charming caresses,
Almost like a love poem.
You see my beloved, today I will not come,
Please, don't be sad.
I know you sit by the fireplace all alone,
Thinking, supporting your head on your hand,
Looking into the glowing fire.
You thought of everything, so nice,
You did everything so nice just for me.
You set the table with the old porcelain,
In a silver tub, a bottle of wine,
And on the table, the white carnations
That now in my absence will wither and die.
In the evening as the cigarettes smoke
and the candles shone
An arousing voice sang my favorite song:

"Why do you pass me by
As if all is over?
As if the happiness we enjoyed
Quickly passed away
Like some little flirtation?"

And then? What would've happened?

We keep silent about that.
Then I would have heard all the words of love that a man can speak.
You see my beloved – I don't want that from you.
You are not the first to possess my heart,
You are not the first who would then forget me,
You are not the first who would leave me.
I know about suffering, I know about hate.
In endless dreams I have gone
Full of hot longing and quiet abandon,
To show the cruel end of happiness,
From this I wanted to spare us.
Do you understand my beloved? Can you forgive?
I am afraid—too afraid, to be happy.

2

SMUGGLING

Bratislava ghetto, Slovakia
• 1942 •

Circumstances were getting grim for the Jews living in Slovakia. Deportations were becoming a common occurrence, and Eva would have heard the rumors of what happened to those taken away by train. Alone in the Bratislava ghetto with an infant, Eva came to the decision that the best chance for her child's survival was for him to be smuggled out and hidden.

Although the exact details of Henrich's removal from the ghetto are murky, Eva claimed that a nurse smuggled her child out. There are similar known accounts of infant rescues across Europe during the Holocaust. One of the most famous child smugglers during the Holocaust, Irena Sendler, a Christian Polish woman, smuggled an estimated 2,500 children out of the Warsaw ghetto during the War. Sendler, in her guise as a nurse and equipped with a city health department badge, would smuggle in much needed items like food and medicine, while sneaking children out (Jones, 2008). Parents found themselves in the gut-wrenching position of choosing whether to keep their children in increasingly dire circumstances or trusting their children to strangers, in hopes of their survival. In cooperation with the Polish underground organization Zegota, Sendler, with a small network of women, smuggled children whose parents were willing to part with them in a myriad of ways. Babies were often given Barbiturate Luminal, an anti-seizure medication with a sedative effect, before being moved. In some cases, Sendler would place a sedated baby in a box that was then loaded onto a truck leaving the ghetto, the box covered up with cargo. Once outside ghetto walls, the infant would be moved to a safe location such as a convent or foster family.

This is the same, heart-wrenching decision Eva faced, and it is very likely that young Henrich was moved out of the ghetto in a very similar fashion. At only seven months old, the risk that his cries would attract attention from ghetto sentries was great. To the unnamed woman who spirited away her child, Eva had one request, "Please let the Engel family know where he is."

Not long after she managed to arrange for her son to be smuggled out of the ghetto, Eva was deported in May 1942 to the Auschwitz concentration camp in Poland.

3

CAPTIVITY

Auschwitz, Poland
• 1943 •

May 15, 1943 Birkenau

Dearest Engl Family,

I have written to you once but even though I have received no answer, I am once again writing to you. You are the only people I still have. How are you? Hopefully you are all well.

How is my beloved child? Do you have any news of my Hanri? I am well and often think of the nice times that I spent when I was with you. How is Laci? How come he doesn't write to me? Has he forgotten me completely? Please write about everything and I will write back promptly. I will be very happy. All of you at home--stay healthy.

Many regards and hand-blown kisses. Write me everything about my beloved Hanri and kiss him for me.

Eva Gisela Pomeranz
Nr. 7747 Block 11, Camp Birkenau

Few details are known about Eva's time in Auschwitz, but what is known points to Eva being a woman of remarkable strength.

In the letter above, we see Eva writing to the Engel family (this name, as with many other names throughout this story, has varied spellings across historical documents). It is interesting to note that she was permitted to send a letter out of Auschwitz, and in this case, it was clearly posted by the Nazis (see a copy of the postcard received and preserved by the Engel family below). In part, it is now known this was part of the Nazis' deception campaign to cover up the human rights atrocities being committed at concentration and work camps throughout Germany and Poland. Some prisoners were allowed to post letters home, although their words were strictly censored. In some cases, prisoners also received mail or parcels from home, but it appears from the letter above that Eva was not receiving any responses to her letters.

What is known about her time at Auschwitz is that, with her talent for languages, Eva was put to work as a translator, and perhaps that sheltered her from more severe work details. Eva spoke Polish, Yiddish, German, Slovak, and Czech and later learned Portuguese and Hebrew. It is believed that Eva was also forced to assist Dr. Josef Mengele, the notorious Nazi doctor and Chief Camp Physician of Auschwitz II (Birkenau), during selections as new transports of prisoners arrived at Auschwitz.

Eva disclosed that the "Angel of Death" would slap her if she did not do her work quickly enough. Eva explained that she would always recognize Mengele, no matter how much he tried to disguise his appearance (after the War it is rumored that Mengele may have had plastic surgery to evade detection and capture).

"I would always know him, just by looking in his eyes," she claimed.

Some of Eva's poems give us meager details of what her life was like in Auschwitz. In one poem, called "My Talk," Eva outlines an exchange with SS camp guard Wilhelm Boger.

In this exchange, Eva makes it clear that there were times camp guards attempted to converse with her, and it took tremendous mental fortitude to bite back her contempt. Boger was a particularly sadistic camp guard who earned the nickname "The Tiger of Auschwitz."

As part of his work in the political department, Boger conducted interrogations on prisoners to maintain the security of the camp, including quelling any internal attempts at resistance by any means deemed necessary. During the course of his interrogations, Boger used torture to extract the information he required. He is known for inventing the "Boger swing," a device for torture which he used to string prisoners upside down. Guards would beat the inverted prisoner across the back and buttocks during questioning until they fainted, only to revive them and begin the beating again. Boger's secretary, Frau Braun, described the atrocity of Boger's work at a later Auschwitz trial in 1959:

"Most perished from the ordeal; some sooner, some later; in the end a sack of bones and flayed flesh and fat was swept along the shambles of that concrete floor to be dragged away," (Kessler, 2019).

Eva's eighteen-year-old cousin was also held at Auschwitz. It was during an Appell, or morning roll call, that her cousin who had lost all hope of survival and already made unsuccessful attempts to take her own life, walked outside without shoes on and was shot and killed as punishment.

A relative of the Engel family reportedly came into contact with Eva at Auschwitz, where she used her gift of languages to intercede for him. The man was selected for the gas chambers, but Eva stepped in and explained that the man was an electrical engineer, and his services might be helpful. The man survived the War due to Eva's intervention and ultimately ended up in Sweden.

In all, Eva was held at Auschwitz until January 1945, when the Soviets began to close in on German-held land, and the end of the War was imminent. Eva was among the thousands of prisoners who were forced on what are now commonly referred to as death marches, as the Nazis desperately attempted to close concentration camps and destroy evidence of what happened within their walls.

Nazi death marches are well documented. It is estimated that in January 1945 there were about 700,000 inmates (Wiener Holocaust Library) held across the entire Nazi concentration camp system, and the Nazis were determined not to let their prisoners fall into Allied or Soviet hands. As the Soviets gained ground on the Eastern front, the Nazis pulled their prisoners deeper into German-held territory.

About 60,000 (Muselia, 2022) prisoners were marched from Auschwitz-Birkenau over 30 miles to a train depot where the survivors were dispersed to other camps throughout the Nazi camp system. On these marches, the malnourished and weak prisoners were forced out into the elements on foot, and if any faltered or fell out of step, they would be shot. It is estimated that 15,000 of the Auschwitz prisoners died on the way to the trains.

The meager bodyweight Eva may have been able to keep on her frame while in Auschwitz would've quickly deteriorated on a forced march in the depths of winter, costing precious calories that wouldn't be replaced.

"Every step in the snow was hard labor. We were exhausted. We grew weaker every day," said Holocaust survivor Herta Goldman in a USC Shoah Foundation interview in a Yad Vashem online exhibit (2015). "You couldn't stop for a minute or step out of line. Whoever stepped out of line got a bullet in the back. I asked a German who passed by me, 'Tell me, where are we going?' He said, 'We have no destination, our purpose is for all of you to drop dead on the way.'"

A uniting theme survivors of these marches note is that their fate was entirely in the hands of the few German guards that accompanied them. March survivors also reported that some of the guards seemed uninformed on what their mission was, were unprepared for the scope of it, and undersupplied.

Holocaust and death march survivor Herta Zauberman, in a 1998 USC Shoah Foundation interview, explained that there was no food provided by the guards on her march. If they were lucky, she said, when they stopped to rest, sometimes local farmers would give them something to eat.

"Day in and day out, every day there were girls shot. It was just a killing field ... I mean hunger, there is no bigger punishment. No killing, and no hitting, and no beating is as painful as hunger," Zauberman said.

To travel from Auschwitz in southern Poland to Ravensbrück in northeastern Germany, Eva and her fellow prisoners had to cover over 400 miles in harrowing conditions. One Holocaust survivor who also survived a march from Auschwitz to Ravensbrück noted that throughout her march her group would stop at different, already-overcrowded camps and outposts for a short while before pushing onward. For the last leg of the journey to Ravensbrück, the prisoners were corralled into open-air cattle cars and shuttled, facing the elements and without food or water, into the camp.

Eva endured all of this without any word about her beloved son.

It is evident in her poem "Ravensbrück" that something changed in Eva after that death march and upon encountering the conditions in the Ravensbrück camp.

My Talk

Oberscharführer Boger– do you know him?
The Devil of Auschwitz –that's what he was called.
He was the head of the political party.
With him there was only hitting, with no recovery.
Once he came in drunk like a pig,
He said, "Eva, come over here,
Today I would like to have a talk with you."
"You with me??? That is a crime!"
"You probably do not know me yet?
Or have you also called me Devil?"
"Yes sir" – was the answer.
He did not say a word to me.
After a while he spoke again.
"Eva. I have heard you sing Hebrew songs.
Were you a Zionist? I read about it somewhere.
Aha! I have received a copy of your
exchange certificate.
Today I would like to have a talk with you.
Speak with me, with this old man.
I would like to speak with the Zionists,
with the big Jewish idealists.
Tell me Eva, if Weitzmann would have come to Hitler
And the two would have started a negotiation
Then the Jews surely would not have come here,
And we Germans would have won the war.
Tell me Eva, you are surely correct. Am I not absolutely right?"

*With a voice sounding hollow and full of anger,
I replied with a smile – "Yes!"*

*"Had the rich not traveled to America,
We could've preserved the peace in Europe.
None of this would have happened had the rich
Not taken all the money with them.
Tell me Eva, you are surely correct. Am I not absolutely right?"*

*With a voice sounding hollow and full of anger,
I replied with a smile – "Yes!"*

*"There are only two peoples that are pure
The Germans and the Jews. Am I correct?"*

*With a voice sounding hollow and full of anger,
I replied with a smile – "Yes!"*

Appell

*Does the howling camp siren also wake you
with its hoarse tone?*

*Do you also stand in your hard drudgery with your teeth
clenched?*

*Do you also stand as I do at the Appell
with spitefully balled fists?*

*Slowly it grows light in the East
When will it come again?*

*Do you have a number like I do,
a number in long rows?*

Do you think of me at the Appell?

And do you also long to be free?

*Do you march out with the columns like many of the
brothers and sisters?*

*Do you long so for home that it burns
in your breast?*

Like today, tomorrow, and yesterday?

*Do you also notice a light in your heart,
a quiet, glad hope?*

*Are you thinking of the coming obligations
when the gates open for us?*

*We would like to go with strength—
freed men and women*

*And when the summer's morning laughs
We will build a better world.*

Ravensbrück

Hopeless landscape – desolate and cold.
Stunted trees that they call a "forest!"
Hardly any grass thrives in the desert sand.
No bell nor the sound of a bird's song in this
Cursed, godforsaken land.
Only ravens and crows caw in the fields.
Behind barbed wire – an inconsolable world.
Behind barbed wire – tormented women like
animals in pens of a slaughterhouse.
Many flourishing lives have withered here.
Many ash-filled urns have been returned home.
And souls are too weak to believe – and doubt
The power of God who witnesses this and
Offers NO HELP.

This is the postcard that Eva sent the Engel family
from Auschwitz.

4
POETESS

Stockholm, Sweden
• 1945 •

While Sweden had claimed neutrality at the outset of the War, by spring 1945 Sweden launched a plan to assist as many survivors of concentration camps as it could. The Swedish Red Cross, headed by Count Greve Folke Bernadotte, secured the release and exchange of around 17,000 concentration camp prisoners, including the last 7,000 women from the Ravensbrück camp. This operation was conducted from March-April 1945 and was the largest rescue effort of concentration camp victims at the tail end of the War.

In March 1945, 250 Swedish soldiers, doctors, and nurses launched into Germany as part of the effort-with Allied air strikes still targeting German cities, it was an extremely dangerous mission. However, Bernadotte met directly with Heinrich Himmler, Hitler's right-hand advisor, on multiple occasions to negotiate the release of prisoners. It is believed that Himmler knew Germany was losing the War and was looking for a way to negotiate peace with the Allies and therefore willing to make concessions. Bernadotte deployed white buses painted with red crosses through Denmark and into Germany, but no safe passage was guaranteed for the mission. It is reported that at least one group of buses was attacked by British Royal Air Force pilots who did not recognize the convoy as a Swedish rescue mission.

As the white buses pulled into Ravensbrück, Eva was able to secure a spot on a bus and get herself, despite the odds, to safety in Sweden. She is listed on a manifest dated August 15, 1945, of prisoners who had been previously transported from Ravensbrück to Sweden in the spring of 1945. When she arrived in Sweden, Eva only weighed 80 pounds and was suffering from malnutrition and general poor health. Sweden provided the backdrop for her respite.

Sometime after her arrival in Sweden, Eva finally learned that her son was still alive. While there, Eva laid plans to be reunited with him. It was still dangerous in Europe for Jews after the War and finding options for getting her son out of Slovakia proved difficult.

There were nurses that took care of the concentration camp evacuees in Sweden, and as the refugees gained their strength, there were distractions and activities to pass the time. Eva got involved in a Yiddish theater in Sweden, where she recited some of the poems included in this book. An article in a Swedish newspaper dated Christmas Eve 1945 features Eva and her poetry, naming her "The Poetess of Auschwitz."

A booklet of her poems was published in Stockholm in 1945. One copy is now housed at the Yad Vashem museum in Jerusalem.

A series of photos also survived from Eva's time in Sweden. One photo features Eva and another young woman dressed in large hats and costumes on a stage draped in background sets. The women are beaming at each other. Another photo features Eva and two other women on a bridge in Sweden on a bright winter day. The women are all smartly dressed and Eva, ever glamorous, sports a handsome fur coat, leather gloves, and a black brimmed hat, tilted just so.

While in Sweden Eva received a letter from a distant cousin who survived the War. He asked her to come join him in Palestine where he'd established a new life (Israel was not yet the independent nation it is today). Eva was convinced it was the best place to start her life after the War and prepared to board a ship for Palestine, leaving Sweden.

Eva, back row, center, with friends in Sweden in 1945.

Eva, on the left in a fur coat, with friends
in Sweden in 1945.

A Swedish newspaper article printed in December 1945 featured Eva's story. The subtitle reads, "The horrors of the camps gave birth to a poet."

Evacuation

In the dark of night I often think
of what you have done to us.
From Auschwitz you sent us to Malchow
Pressed one hundred of us in a wagon.
To each of the one hundred you gave
two destinations
And sent us away, away from the East.
So we traveled hungry, cold and dirty
All across Germany.
The way led to Ravensbrück,
There we were still a bit round and thick,
We were sent to the youth camp,
There we quickly became slim and skinny.
From there to the Malchow "Paradise,"
Where I could hardly stand on my own feet.
So I ask myself in the dark night,
What have you done to us?
You robbed us of love, destroyed our faith
You have only done one thing, you have
taught us hate.

To my Son

My sweet little son, you know nothing of this,
That I, in far away Sweden—
Over you hold my motherly hand at every hour of the day.
The wound in my heart opens wide.
I picture you big in front of my eyes.
It makes me want to scream, I am almost wild.
But you, my little son, you know nothing of this ...
You must enjoy your childhood now ...
There will come a time when I will be rid of this hard burden,
And to you I will return.
Then we both will be filled with joy.
Be calm my little one, do not make sad faces.
For then I will NEVER, EVER leave you again.

To the Swedish Nation

Very often I deal with the thought of:
How can we thank you?
It is so important, yet I think it is impossible.
For all that you have done for us,
You can not give thanks all at one time.
You have to do it all your life and never
shy away from doing it.
Do you realize what you have done for us?
You took us out of hell and brought us
to paradise.
You treated us as if we were sick children.
You asked us daily if we were feeling healthier.
You were all so wonderful—you are
the ideal people.
Once we leave here, it is with joy that
we will remember this place.
Our loving thoughts will always be with you.
Whatever will be our destiny,
For you, we will always have a hearty,
"Thank you very much!" – "Tack sa mycket!"

5

Juraj

Bratislava, Slovakia
• 1946 •

In a series of cracked black and white photos, a family poses expectantly for a Christmastime portrait session. In one photo, a fair-haired teenage girl stands behind her family beside a tinsel-draped Christmas tree, while in front, a little boy dressed in a sailor's uniform is flanked by a man and woman. In yet another photo, the little boy, with his shining hair well coiffed and sailor's uniform pressed, sits alone holding the reins of a handsome, spotted rocking horse.

In the photos, most likely snapped in 1946, the Prissigens- Jan and Magdalena, their daughter Magda, and a son with deep set hazel eyes-appear the epitome of familial warmth, memorializing the holidays on film.

In the Protestant Prissigen household the youngest member's name was Juraj, a boy who was much beloved by his family. The family had their own way of saying his name—they called him "Jurek."

At five years old, Juraj led the happy life of a child.

Paperwork later uncovered listed Magdalena Prissigen as Juraj's godmother, although to him she was the only mother he'd ever known.

Little Juraj, after his removal from the ghetto as an infant, was dropped at a Protestant church by the nurse who spirited him away, and he was then given to a rural farming family. The farming family kept young Juraj until the end of the War in a town called Nove Mesto nad Vahom, north of Bratislava. Nothing further is known about the family Juraj stayed with for three years.

The Engel family, who had grown close to Eva in her time working for them, did not forget their promise to Eva to keep looking for her son. When they traced the little boy to the farm, he appeared small and undernourished. The Engels decided to remove little Juraj until Eva could be reunited with him. They'd arranged for Juraj to come back to Bratislava and live with a family who also knew Eva –the Prissigen family.

The Prissigens had two family dogs; one white German shepherd called Lord, and one dachshund that Juraj adored. He also loved to climb a cherry tree that graced the backyard and harvest its sweet fruit.

Fully integrated into the family, young Juraj was sometimes sent across the street to a pub to tote large mugs of beer back for parties at the Prissigen residence.

One detail his foster sister Magda revealed 60 years later was that, as a boy, Juraj never cried–even when he first arrived.

For Juraj Prissigen, hiding in plain sight was easy because it was the only life he could remember.

Juraj, middle, flanked by the Prissigen family at Christmastime in 1946.

Juraj in the Prissigen household in 1946.

Juraj with Magdalena Prissigen.

The Prissigen family in 1946.

6

INTERNMENT

Cyprus
• 1947 •

As Eva was finally on her way to start a new life in a new country, Palestine, and closer to arranging for her son to join her, the inexplicable happened.

When she boarded a ship, no doubt filled with other Jewish refugees from Europe headed for the Middle East, it appeared she was leaving the War's impacts behind with the promise of a new life ahead of her.

But as her vessel, named The Eilat, neared the shores of Palestine, it was cut off and intercepted by the British Royal Navy.

There is political context as to why this happened. Following the end of World War I, the British held control of Palestine under a League of Nations mandate. They held a presence there, according to the Balfour Declaration, which assured the establishment of a Jewish national homeland in Palestine. However, a white paper published by the British government in 1939 complicated this promise by also pledging the establishment of an independent Palestinian state within 10 years and restricting Jewish immigration to 75,000 over the next five years.

Ultimately, both the Jewish population already in Israel and the Palestinian Arabs living there rejected the white paper, opposing Britain's plan for the mandate. Britain wanted to politically appease Arab interests in the Middle East, which was impossible to do without failing to fulfill promises already made to Jews.

And while in the interwar period, British military actions in Palestine were mostly opposite Arab militants who opposed Jewish immigration (such as the Arab Revolt 1936-1939), British troops also faced armed resistance from Zionist groups.

It was in this environment of conflict and ongoing uncertainty in the outcome of how Palestine would be partitioned after the War that Eva's vessel neared the mandate of Palestine.

Once intercepted by the British, Eva and the refugees aboard her ship were redirected to the island of Cyprus, where they were held in an internment camp. After the War, the British interred more than 50,000 refugees on the Crown colony island.

Eva was behind barbed wire again.

In a Times of Israel article (Martell, 2021), Holocaust survivor Rose Lipszyc described her experience being detained on Cyprus.

"The English soldiers — who I would have kissed the feet of for liberating me in Germany — were leaping into our little boat with batons," she said. "The English weren't starving us, and they weren't killing us like the Germans. But it was so traumatic, that the very same people who had freed me just a short time ago now incarcerated me."

Surviving footage from the camps in Cyprus shows rows of canvas tents walled by barbed wire. Metal half-dome structures serving as housing dot the skyline, providing little shelter from the elements. Young detainees can be seen sporting shorts and rolled sleeves doing calisthenics and group physical fitness in the desert-like terrain.

Charity organizations were aware of the refugees' conditions in Cyprus and were permitted to sponsor activities for them including schooling, health care, and vocational training. One surviving photo shows refugees learning sewing on machines lined up inside a metal hut.

There are several surviving photos from Eva's time on Cyprus. In one black and white photo she leans a shoulder against a corrugated, white-washed building. Dressed in pleated shorts, a button-down collared short-sleeve shirt, and Mary Jane-style sandals with socks, she's stylish despite her circumstances. Her blonde hair is styled in short curls resting on her shoulders, brushed away from her face.

Another photo shows Eva in a midriff-baring white ensemble with the initials "EW" embroidered on her top. Others show her posing with friends next to thick barbed wire fences with a guard tower looming in the back. Still other photographs feature Eva surrounded by groups of friends, all smiling and looking in generally good spirits despite their status. In all photos Eva appears outwardly healthy to the casual viewer. But the photos don't tell the story about the mental strain of the losses she experienced, being separated from her son, and the longing to see him again.

A poem Eva wrote, "A Letter to the Jewish Mothers," described some of the feelings she struggled with during this time.

In 1947, the United Nations adopted Resolution 181, the plan to divide Palestine along Jewish and Palestinian borders. Then finally, after Eva was held for a year in captivity on Cyprus, the creation of Israel as an autonomous nation occurred in May 1948.

The birth of Israel as a nation-state also marked the end of the British Mandate. As the British pulled out, Eva was finally allowed to enter the newly-recognized nation of Israel. Eva was reunited with the relative who had sent for her and she was finally free to live life on her own terms.

But her dream of being reunited with the son she longed to embrace was delayed once again.

For Eva, war seemed to follow her. As soon as the British Mandate ended, the 1948 Arab-Israeli War began. Eva arrived in Israel as armies from Lebanon, Syria, Iraq, and Egypt launched an assault on Israeli-held sectors of the former Mandate.

Because it was unsafe, again she was made to wait to see her son.

After almost a decade apart, separated by wars, racism, borders, and rows of barbed wire, when the fighting ceased in 1949, Eva was finally able to start the process of sending for the son she'd said goodbye to in the Bratislava ghetto.

A Letter to the Jewish Mothers

Jewish mothers of the little European world
What did you actually do
That you now have to suffer so?
Could you not have avoided all of this?
They have brought you into the camps,
Everything removed that you ever had …
Even the dearest to you on God's earth.
What will become of you now?
They have taken your children, the children were taken.
The heart is torn, the soul is melted away.
And now you are free—you must live on.
For whom is the work? For whom is the aspiration?
Now you must not forget,
You must carry the banner of heroines.
Even if you are weak and the tears swell in your throat,
You are the heroines.
The quiet heroines in the new world!

There is no Friendship

*If you believe that you have found friends
That are bound to you with heart and soul
That during good and bad situations
For them, as well as for you, you will find
a position.
That you, in your entire life
Would give everything of yours for them.
If you think it is so nice,
Then go on, believe your false illusions!
For it only depends on the positions!*

*When you are up in life, then you certainly
have friends.
But when the wheel turns another way,
Will someone then still understand?
There is no friendship idealism,
There is only bad materialism.
So have no false illusions
If you need friends—find a position.*

Eva and a friend in a British internment camp on Cyprus.

Eva in an internment camp.

Eva in an internment camp.

Eva, second from right, with contemporaries in a British internment camp.

Eva in an internment camp.

7

THE RABBI

Bratislava, Slovakia
• 1948 •

It was already dark on the evening Juraj Prissigen's life changed dramatically. Two men in long black coats and hats appeared at the Prissigen residence insisting Juraj come with them. A shroud of grief covered the house with their arrival.

No one explained to Juraj what was happening, and he didn't know why he had to leave with the strange men.

He was certain the men were there to take him away from his family.

The Prissigens packed a small suitcase for Juraj with his belongings and handed him his stuffed teddy bear.

Jan and Magdalena Prissigen were visibly upset, yet his foster family had no choice but to let him go. For seven-year-old Juraj, he was being taken away from the only parents he knew and none of the adults would tell him why.

The Prissigens simply embraced him and told him not to lose his suitcase because it carried all of his possessions in the world.

Then they let him go.

The two men took Juraj in the dark to a train station where, after boarding a train, Juraj didn't sleep all night. With the suitcase propped on his lap and in the company of strangers, he clutched onto his belongings, making sure he didn't lose a single item, as his parents had warned.

When the train reached its destination, the two men escorted Juraj to a Jewish orphanage. It was Juraj's first time meeting other children like him, although he didn't know initially that they were all refugees waiting to be reunited with their parents.

Eva, it turns out, had been in contact with an organization formed by the audacious British Rabbi Solomon Schonfeld to go collect her son.

In her book, "The Hide-and-Seek Children," (2012) author Barbara Barnett paints an in-depth picture of the rabbi who worked tirelessly to save as many Jewish children as possible from post-war Europe.

Rabbi Schonfeld is described as a dashing, charismatic character who many found it hard to believe was a rabbi at all. He was described as intelligent and daring and proved to be a man responsible for rescuing about 5,000 people in total.

Rabbi Schonfeld took on a mantle of responsibility at a young age.

When Solomon Schonfeld's father, Rabbi Victor Schonfeld, died suddenly in 1929, the Adath Yisroel Synagogue in North London voted that young Schonfeld, despite being only 17 years old, would take over as rabbi in his father's place. Schonfeld, already enrolled in a law program at the London School of Economics, abandoned his plans to enter the legal profession. A more experienced rabbi took over his father's congregation while Schonfeld completed his rabbinical studies in Slovakia and Lithuania. In

1933, at age 21, Schonfeld returned to London to take up his post as rabbi of his father's synagogue and principal of the Avigdor High School. The Schonfelds' schooling theory was one of blending together secular and religious education, which eliminated the need for Hebrew school (also called Cheder).

Having spent time outside of the U.K. for his rabbinical education, Schonfeld had been victim to an anti-Semitic attack himself, and witnessed attacks on others. He, perhaps more than many in the U.K., understood the dire situation Jews faced in Europe. Even before the War began, Schonfeld began petitioning to rescue Jews from the European interior.

In 1938 Schonfeld became director of the Chief Rabbi's Religious Emergency Council (CRREC), which was registered as a war charity. Through this organization, Schonfeld worked tirelessly to acquire visas for Jewish religious leaders and children, bringing them to the U.K. before the War.

Schonfeld's first transport of unaccompanied children to the U.K. came from Vienna in 1938. With each unaccompanied child Schonfeld sponsored, the U.K. required a host family to receive them and proper documentation for their stay in Britain. Schonfeld's work also required ongoing funding, which he never tired petitioning for.

Schonfeld attempted to secure traditional means to protect Jewish victims of the Holocaust, like petitioning the British government to intervene, and alternately very unconventional methods, such as buying a small island in the Bahamas and a castle in Ireland to house Jewish refugees.

Schonfeld went on missions into antisemitic territory after the War, extracting Jewish survivors from both displaced persons camps set up after the

War, and gentile homes. He went on these missions into Europe in a car accompanied by armored guards, wearing a uniform that he'd fashioned himself. "He did the most amazing things in order to get those children out ... To us, he was a god," said Lili Pohlmann (nee Stern), another of the children who accompanied Rabbi Schonfeld on a transport (Association of Jewish Refugees, Refugee Voices Archive, 2022). "A god came & took us out. He invented this uniform for himself. Now, what an idea is that? It looked like an English officer. Why did he do that? Because he thought if he goes dressed in civilian clothes or as a rabbi he may not survive. And if he does, nobody would even listen to him. But the Poles love a military uniform. So he invented this magnificent uniform. And his cap had Jewish insignias on it but nobody would look. Nobody knew."

More than once, Schonfeld survived assassination attempts. For Schonfeld, he saw rescuing displaced children from the European interior and the future of Judaism as one and the same. As such, he was adamant that children rescued in his organization receive an Orthodox education. In a pamphlet he wrote in 1944, Schonfeld urged that Jewish refugees in Great Britain not be alienated from the religion of Judaism. For Schonfeld, this was about preservation of the culture; he wanted to make sure those who had escaped physical annihilation would also survive cultural annihilation.

As such, when he brought unaccompanied Jewish children from the European interior who did not have a particular sponsored home to go to, he housed them in group settings. In these group settings he fashioned the children's environment after the Avigdor High School where religion was woven into every part of the children's day--even for the children who learned by surprise that they were Jewish.

A website dedicated to child survivors of the Holocaust, the '45 Aid society, states that Rabbi Schonfeld was a "man of action and not paper trails." Often there were very narrow windows of access to unaccompanied children in Europe. Diplomatic red tape in various countries forced documents to be altered, and Schonfeld was willing to do whatever it took to rescue as many Jewish children as possible. Schonfeld and his helpers changed names, birthdates, and nationalities on paperwork to transport children back to the U.K. It is for this reason that the trail of his work is laden with often intended inaccuracies. For Juraj, that meant that his name was hurriedly changed to "Gyorgy" on Rabbi Schonfeld's paperwork to bypass Slovakian officials' suspicion that Slovakian nationals were being removed from the country.

Newly-named Gyorgy then embarked on a voyage across Europe with Rabbi Schonfeld's organization. Gyorgy traveled with a large group of 148 total children by train from Bratislava which took them through Czechoslovakia, Germany, and Holland. For the first time, Gyorgy found himself surrounded by dozens of unaccompanied children, all speaking different European languages. In Holland the children took a ferry to Dover, England where Gyorgy was served his very first British tea.

From Dover the group traveled to London, where a number of Rabbi Schonfeld's rescued children found homes to sponsor them. The group stayed in London for about 10 days. But Gyorgy, along with 99 other children, were left without permanent placement.

Gyorgy, circled, with a group of children at Ohel David Children's Home, where he stayed temporarily in the process of being moved from Slovakia to the UK.

Gyorgy, as he was called for a short time, is circled in this group photo where he is with other refugee children rescued by Rabbi Solomon Schonfeld.

8

THE CASTLE

Ireland
• 1948 •

Newly re-named Gyorgy, as one of Rabbi Schonfeld's refugee children, was rapidly thrust into a world of Orthodox Judaism. While with the Prissigens, Gyorgy lived as a Slovakian Protestant boy and Judaism was as foreign to him as a language he had never heard. It was now clear to Gyorgy, however, that he was expected to assimilate Jewish culture quickly; this was his new life.

Little Gyorgy's first real taste of Jewish culture was in London, where he experienced a Passover celebration.

Rabbi Schonfeld, however, knew he could not stay indefinitely in London with 100 children—something had to be done to find them permanent accommodations until they could be reunited with surviving family or were old enough to live independently.

The Rabbi worked tirelessly in London to secure donations and lodging for the children.

Finally, arrangements were made for a visa for the 100 children to stay in Ireland for a period of one year. Schonfeld, with his powers of persuasion and determination, partnered with wealthy Jewish pharmacist and optician, Jacob Levy, who graciously offered to foot the bill for the children's residence in Ireland.

In 1947, Mr. Levy purchased a 17-room, late 1800s estate called Clonyn Castle (alternately called Delvin Castle), about 50 miles outside of Dublin for the children. Records show that the castle was purchased for a sum of £30,000.

Soon Gyorgy, along with 99 other children, boarded a ship for Ireland, and he found himself at the sprawling, 1,600-acre estate.

At the castle with its turrets, grand entryway, and marble staircase, Gyorgy began his induction in earnest into the Jewish Orthodox faith.

The first order of business for Gyorgy was to look the part of an Orthodox boy. For the first time he was given traditional Jewish clothing, taught to grow out the sidelocks of his hair (Peyot), and how to wear a prayer shawl.

Next was a Bris, or ceremonial circumcision, to officially welcome him into the faith. Details left by Mrs. Olga Eppel, the Clonyn administrator, document Gyorgy's visit to a clinic for a Bris. Mrs. Eppel recounted the event in "The Hide and Seek Children":

"Young Gyorgy Prissigen, whose age we could only guess as six because he still had his baby teeth, had to be initiated into the covenant of Abraham [i.e. to be circumcised]. He entered Portabello Nursing Home as Gyorgy Prissigen, the name he got from his non-Jewish foster parents. He came out of the nursing home as Avrom Dov, the name I gave him, after my late father."

-Mrs. Eppel

Now circumcised, the boy who was once called Henrich, Juraj, and Gyorgy, had fully become Avrom Dov.

Leaning on his pre-war experience of running religious-centric schools, one of Rabbi Schonfeld's top priorities at Clonyn Castle was education. Schonfeld assigned Rabbi Israel Cohen and his wife Trudi to take over running the castle; Rabbi Cohen as principal of the school, and his wife tending to health and domestic matters.

The children received prayer books, attended services twice per day, taught how to pray in the Orthodox way, and learned subjects like English and Jewish history. There was also ample opportunity for the children to participate in leisure activities, like playing soccer on the lawn.

As one of the youngest children at Clonyn Castle, Avrom was assigned one of the older girls to tend to him. Unfortunately, the teen, who had survived her own traumas during the War, was cruel to him.

The girl spanked Avrom often, and he wasn't sure why.

Otherwise, Avrom's stay at the castle was pleasant. He had a room on the second floor facing the front, and Avrom enjoyed his extravagant accommodations.

Life at the Irish castle went on for little Avrom Dov for nine months until one day he was informed he would be leaving Ireland.

On January 24, 1949, Avrom Dov and about 25 other children boarded a bus that would take them to the Dublin airport. The group flew to Paris, where they took a train to Marseille, France.

Avrom Dov had no understanding of where he was going or why–no one had explained to him why he had to travel to Israel.

After about ten days in Marseille, the children were granted passage on an Israeli ship headed for Haifa. The journey oversea took about one week. Avrom had a horrible case of motion sickness during the trip and vomited along the way. The children were given chocolates to calm their stomachs, but for Avrom, the sweets didn't help.

When Avrom's group docked in Kiryat Haim, Israel, he was taken to a holding camp where he stayed about a week.

It really wasn't clear to him that he was in another country or what this new location meant–he went where he was told.

He was housed with other children and was fed hard brown bread with cold butter which he smeared with his finger when he couldn't find a knife.

One evening a tall gentleman with a mustache wearing an Israeli military uniform approached him in the holding camp and lifted Avrom up into his arms. The man told him, "Now I'm going to take you to your mother."

Avrom boarded a bus with the man, and they traveled to Tel Aviv where Eva was living. Avrom Dov soon learned the man who met him in the camp was his adoptive father–his mother's relative and new husband–Sigmund Weiser.

Avrom Dov had no memory of this woman, Eva, and he wasn't sure how he was supposed to feel, being told that a stranger was his mother. For Avrom, it was all very strange.

The woman he encountered spoke to him in Slovak, a language they could both understand.

The moment Eva had longed for for so long had finally come, yet truly, they were strangers at first. It was at the same time a long-awaited and bittersweet reunion: the joy of being reunited was surely complicated by the years of distance War had wedged between them.

That first night he spent with his mother, she took his Orthodox clothing away and told him he wouldn't need it anymore. The next day, Eva took him to the barber to cut off his sidelocks–in Israel he wouldn't play the role of Avrom Dov. Before long she gave him a new name: Yoram.

For Me the War Is Lost

The British, Russians, and Americans
Were victorious over the Japanese and Germans
The Allied soldiers fought valiantly like lions
Their blood flowed, but the war ended well,
very well.
Even though a lot of blood was shed,
there was a glorious victory
At the end of a difficult war.
For me, personally, it does not matter.
I can only say—
There was once a difficult war that ended
in a great victory.

For me it makes no difference,
it is all the same.
They have taken everything away from me.
I lost my parents, brothers, family and home.
I was left like a church mouse—in the world
all alone.

For us Jews, the war is not won.
The war against us continues, and we are continually
conquered.
How can we expect the homeless who have lost
everything to feel the joy of victory?
What is life for me? What does this victory mean to me?
I have lost EVERYTHING.
For me ... THE WAR IS LOST.

Avrom Dov on the steps of Clonyn Castle in Ireland with other refugee children.

Clonyn Castle, where Avrom Dov lived for about a year and learned to practice Orthodox Judaism while under the care of Rabbi Solomon Schonfeld.

Avrom Dov with two of Schonfeld's older wards in Ireland.

9

HOMECOMING

Tel Aviv, Israel
• 1958 •

Sitting at the kitchen table wearing a billowy black polka dot blouse with a large white bow tied in the front, cigarette smoke encircled Eva's head while a glass of brandy sat in close range of her right hand. Taking in the sight of his mother, 17-year-old Yoram smiled.

Eva gestured to the empty seat next to her, implying Yoram should sit down. Her blonde hair was coiffed in face-framing waves. She told Yoram she had a new joke for him.

Yoram moved toward the table, ready for yet another of his mother's humorous stories.

Fanning smoke away from his face with his hand, Yoram muttered a half-serious complaint he had offered up many times before. "Always smoking," he protested.

Eva reminded him that in the camps the only thing she had to smoke was the ends of other people's finished cigarettes off the ground.

"You want me to quit smoking when I can afford to buy a pack of cigarettes?" his mother quipped.

And that's how the conversation went every time. Any time Eva's constant smoking was questioned she would bring up the camps and what she had endured there. After liberation, she would allow herself the luxury to smoke, full stop. And with that rebuttal, the conversation would be over.

The new joke she'd encountered was from the latest German book she was reading. Her appetite for reading was insatiable. She had already worked her way through all of the books she cared to read in the Polish library in Tel Aviv and was now making a dent in the German library's stocks.

They both threw their heads back and laughed at Eva's joke; to Yoram, his mother's humor was one of his favorite things about her.

A scar only a few years old on her left forearm peeked out of her blouse when she lifted her fluted brandy glass to take a drink. Pink and puckered, the scar served as a reminder of the number that was once there in thick, black ink: 7747.

"I don't want to be a number again," Eva told her son again.

Yoram asked her, as he'd asked many times if she would ever tell him everything–what really happened to her during the War.

"I'm trying to bury it, and you're trying to dig it up," Eva told her son, like she had told him before.

Yoram simply nodded his head in acceptance, his hazel eyes connecting with hers. He allowed his mother to keep the secrets she wasn't ready to tell. The life they enjoyed together was enough.

* * * *

Jerry and Eva later in life.

Jerry holding an image of Eva after her passing by photographer Marissa Roth as part of her photo series "Witness to Truth" for the Simon Wiesenthal Center/ Museum of Tolerance in Los Angeles.

AUTHOR'S NOTE

I discovered Jerry (Henrich) Weiser's story through a virtual talk he gave in 2020 for the Museum of Tolerance in Los Angeles. At the time, I was taking in as many Holocaust survivor's stories as I could manage while doing research for my historical fiction novel on two Polish survivors. Watching him tell his story, I was transfixed: I had to know more. He and Eva's story was unique from others I'd read–from Auschwitz to Ireland, Sweden and Cyprus–their survival and reunification defied odds. As a parent myself, I was not only struck by the colossal decision to give up a child when faced with grave uncertainty, but also the unifying thread throughout their story of a dream deferred amongst continued setbacks.

I reached out to the Museum of Tolerance, and they were kind enough to connect me with Jerry. I enjoyed a several hours-long interview with Jerry and his gracious wife, Rita, in their home in Los Angeles. They presented me with carefully-preserved documents and photographs, and the history of Eva and Jerry's survival, patched together after her passing.

One of the great mysteries central to Jerry and Eva's story is Jerry's true parentage. While she was still alive, Eva never revealed to her son that the man he thought was his father, was not. It wasn't until after she passed away that his adoptive father, Sigmund, disclosed Jerry's biological father had perished in the Holocaust. There is only one surviving document that names Jerry's father as "Frantisek Kohn," and it is a hand-written account by a temporary guardian when he was being moved after the War. I underscore again that documents like this were populated with false information regularly to secure movement for refugees around Europe. Despite my own research efforts and employment of a Polish consultant to search archives in Poland, we were unable to find any further information about this person, Frantisek Kohn. My frustration as a researcher in being unable to bring more clarity to Jerry about his own life and lineage stands as a powerful reminder of how much was lost during the Holocaust: not only people, not only families, but the loss of personal histories.

I also want to call attention to what else we don't know about this story. That speaks just as loudly as the details we do. Eva kept much of what happened to her during the Holocaust hidden away. Her poems give us a glimpse into both the turmoil and jubilance she experienced, but palpably, her own full account is missing. Like a lot of others who survived WWII, she didn't discuss what happened. Eva told her son to look in her closet after she passed away and he would find a box that contained details about the Holocaust. So, it was only after she died that Jerry discovered the box and learned about the 11 original poems included in this book and other details about both of their lives he had never been told.

It is said that poetry is activism: it's revolutionary in its own right. My hope is that by ensuring Eva's full body of work is published, the poems will give her the voice she didn't have while in captivity and when so much was taken from her. By honoring her art, we safeguard a tiny piece of what the oppressor attempted to annihilate.

Jerry eventually became accustomed to life in Israel and while there were lean years initially, his parents eventually became owners of a popular Tel Aviv restaurant called The Dolphin. Nights spent alone in a room rented out of another family's home while his parents worked at the restaurant turned into nights at home with his mother in a two-bedroom apartment they purchased near the restaurant as The Dolphin gained success.

Jerry described his mother as a non-religious person after the War–she'd lost her faith. Jerry, however, continued practicing Judaism throughout his adulthood and passed the religion on to his two sons Michael and Daniel, and three grandchildren Sam, Eli, and Jonah. Jerry and Rita emigrated to the United States in 1975 and lived in Los Angeles where Jerry continued to give talks, telling his story at museums, to students, and wherever else he was able. Jerry explained that having descendants to pass his family name onto was in a way his own vengeance for what had been done to the Jews of Europe—his way of proving that the Nazis failed in their plan of eradicating all Jews.

One thing he did for himself as an adult in America that he was never able to as a child: choose his own name. His other five identities had been given to him, this one he chose for himself: Jerry.

Sadly, Jerry passed away in October 2022, just before the completion of this book. My hope is that his and Eva's legacy live on through this book as well as the lessons that can be learned from what they endured.

ACKNOWLEDGEMENTS

I would like to thank Jerry Weiser, his lovely wife, Rita, and their entire family for trusting me with this story. Big thanks also goes to the Museum of Tolerance and other historical organizations like Yad Vashem that are committed to preserving and safeguarding the stories of the Holocaust into the collective consciousness. Finally, I'd like to thank my late mother, Florence Jane Hemmerly-Brown, who never stopped encouraging me to write.

REFERENCES

Barnett, B. 2012. *The Hide-and-Seek Children: Recollections of Jewish Survivors from Slovakia.* Mansion Field.

Conway, J. (1974). The Churches, the Slovak State and the Jews 1939-1945. *The Slavonic and East European Review, 52*(126), 85-112. Retrieved May 26, 2021, from http://www.jstor.org/stable/4206836

Jelinek, Y. (1971). Storm-Troopers in Slovakia: The Rodobrana and the Hlinka Guard. *Journal of Contemporary History, 6*(3), 97-119. Retrieved May 8, 2021, from http://www.jstor.org/stable/259881

Jones, M. (2008, December 4). The Smuggler. *New York Times.* https://www.nytimes.com/2008/12/28/magazine/28sendler-t.html

Kessler, J. (2021, October 24). Frau Braun and The Tiger of Auschwitz. *California Literary Review.* https://calitreview.com/frau-braun-and-the-tiger-of-auschwitz/

Martell, P. (2021, August 10). 75 years on, harsh British detention of Holocaust survivors in Cyprus remembered. *Times of Israel.* https://www.timesofisrael.com/75-years-on-harsh-british-detention-of-holocaust-survivors-in-cyprus-remembered/

Muselia. (2022). *Auschwitz. Not Long Ago. Not Far Away.* https://auschwitz.net/en/

Newsweek. (2015, May 14). *The Swedish Schindler: How Count Bernadotte saved thousands of Jews from death.* https://www.newsweek.com/swedish-schindler-how-count-bernadotte-saved-thousands-jews-death-327234

Schnitker, H. (2011, October 24). *Inside the Church during WWII Catholicism, Nationalism and Nazism amongst the Czechs, Slovaks and Hungarians.* Catholic News Agency. https://www.catholicnewsagency.com/column/51659/catholicism-nationalism-and-nazism-amongst-the-czechs-slovaks-and-hungarians

The Weiner Holocaust Library. (2021). *Death Marches: Evidence and Memory.* https://wienerholocaustlibrary.org/exhibition/death-marches-evidence-and-memory/

United States Holocaust Memorial Museum. (2022). United States Holocaust Memorial Museum. (nd.) *Holocaust Encyclopedia: Tarnow.* https://encyclopedia.ushmm.org/content/en/article/tarnow

USC Shoah Foundation Institute testimony of Herta Zauberman. (1998, November 18). *Herta Zauberman.* https://collections.ushmm.org/search/catalog/vha48198

Yad Vashem. (2015, March 8). *Holocaust survivor Herta Goldman talks about escaping from the death march.* https://www.youtube.com/watch?v=iBXjz6RxWQY

ABOUT THE AUTHOR

Alexandra Hays is a regional Emmy-nominated author, storyteller, and graduate of Elon University's Journalism program. She was born in Blue Hill, Maine and has served in the U.S. Army since 2004 where her journalistic writing has been published and recognized nationally. She writes historical fiction and non-fiction with a passion for stories of survival and resilience.